ASK THE CONSTITUTION

Can Certain Religions Be Outlawed?

Ty Schalter

Enslow Publishing
101 W. 23rd Street
Suite 240
New York, NY 10011
USA

enslow.com

Published in 2020 by Enslow Publishing, LLC.
101 W. 23rd Street, Suite 240, New York, NY 10011

Library of Congress Cataloging-in-Publication Data

Names: Schalter, Ty, author.
Title: Can certain religions be outlawed? / Ty Schalter.
Description: New York : Enslow Publishing, 2020. | Series: Ask the Constitution | Includes bibliographical references and index. | Audience: Grade 5 to 8.
Identifiers: LCCN 2018051348| ISBN 9781978507104 (library bound) | ISBN 9781978508392 (pbk.)
Subjects: LCSH: Freedom of religion—United States—Juvenile literature. | United States.
Constitution 1st Amendment—Juvenile literature.
Classification: LCC BR516 .S34 2020 | DDC 323.44/20973—dc23
LC record available at https://lccn.loc.gov/2018051348

Printed in the United States of America

To Our Readers: We have done our best to make sure all website addresses in this book were active and appropriate when we went to press. However, the author and the publisher have no control over and assume no liability for the material available on those websites or on any websites they may link to. Any comments or suggestions can be sent by email to customerservice@enslow.com.

Photo Credits: Cover and p. 1 top, interior pages background (Constitution) Jack R Perry Photography/Shutterstock.com, cover, p. 1 (interfaith symbols) Godong/robertharding/Getty Images; p. 5 Olivier Douliery/Getty Images; p. 7 Lambert/Hulton Fine Art Collection/Getty Images; p. 8 Print Collector/Hulton Archive/Getty Images; p. 9 MPI/Archive Photos/Getty Images; p. 12 Stock Montage/Archive Photos/Getty Images; p. 16 Alex Wong/Getty Images; p. 18 Hulton Deutsch/Corbis Historical/Getty Images; p. 20 iofoto/Shutterstock.com; p. 23 Keep Smiling Photography/Shutterstock.com; p. 24 L.E.Mormile/Shutterstock.com; p. 25 Larry St. Pierre/Shutterstock.com; p. 28 Tom DeCicco/Shutterstock.com; p. 32 Zach Gibson/Getty Images; p. 34 Andrew Caballero-Reynolds/AFP/Getty Images; p. 37 Hyoung Chang/Denver Post/Getty Images; cover, interior pages (paper scroll) Andrey_Kuzmin/Shutterstock.com.

Contents

Introduction

Do you think you can handle the Three-Pronged Lemon Challenge? It sounds like a YouTube dare, but it's actually the way the United States government checks to make sure its laws don't interfere with anyone's religious freedom.

You might have heard that phrase "religious freedom" a lot lately. It's been in the news for many different reasons. Some people think the government is stopping religion from being as important a part of American life as it used to be. Others are afraid the government might impose a specific religion (or the rules of a specific religion) on them. Still others are worried the government will make their faith illegal.

These thoughts are really scary. But does the government have that kind of power?

The first words of the First Amendment of the Constitution of the United States of America are "Congress shall make no law respecting an establishment of religion."[1] That sounds like the government can't make any rules about religion at all.

But read those words again. Just because Congress can't pass a law establishing a religion, does that really mean everybody gets to worship however they want? What happens when one person's freedom of religion gets in the way of somebody else's?

Questions like these are at the heart of several recent court cases, some of which have been heard by the Supreme Court of the United States. In one, a baker refused to make a wedding cake for a same-sex couple, claiming it was against his religious beliefs.[2] In another, President Donald Trump signed orders stopping immigration from several majority-Muslim

We often hear that "freedom of religion" is guaranteed by the US Constitution. But what does the Constitution really say—and what beliefs are really protected?

countries.[3] Former attorney general Jeff Sessions formed a "religious liberty task force"[4] to make sure the court hears more cases like these—and the boundaries of our rights are tested more often.

How will the justices respond to different groups testing the limits of religious freedom in school, at work, and in public life? The same way they decide other cases: by reading the Constitution, thinking about what the people who wrote it intended, and considering past court decisions.

The "Lemon Test" came from a 1971 Supreme Court ruling, *Lemon v. Kurtzman*. The court's opinion contained three principles for deciding future religious-freedom issues. The Lemon Test isn't perfect, and it isn't the only thing the court considers. But it's a useful way to figure out whether Congress has made a law that infringes on one of our most important personal freedoms.

As we go through the history of laws and court cases dealing with religious freedom, before and after *Lemon v. Kurtzman*, we'll better understand how the court might rule on current and upcoming cases—and what its decisions will mean for our future. Could the government really outlaw a religion? Let's ask the Constitution!

The First Amendment

Even after declaring their independence and winning a war against England together, the thirteen colonies that became the United States didn't agree on how their new nation should work. There was a long fight to adopt the original Constitution and a long list of proposed amendments to make it better.

From before the Continental Congress to the adoption of the Bill of Rights, many key Founders—not to mention regular citizens—worried about how their new nation would protect their religious freedom.

Religious "Flee"dom

Lots of people who tell the story of America start with the Pilgrims. We know they came over on the *Mayflower*, founded what would become Massachusetts, and celebrated their survival in America with a feast we now call Thanksgiving.

But why did they leave England?

The Pilgrims were Puritan separatists, meaning they thought the official Church of England had gone so wrong, they had to get away from it completely. When the leader of the country is also the leader of the church,

The Pilgrims took the hard journey to America because they wanted the freedom to worship their own way.

The Puritans wanted their way of life to be an example for the rest of the world.

speaking out against the church means speaking out against the king. Independent churches were made illegal in 1593, and meeting for church services could be punished by jail—or even death. [1]

The Pilgrims left England in 1609, moving to Holland, where they could worship in peace, but moved again in 1620—this time to America, so they could worship the way they wanted *and* preserve their English culture.

The Plymouth Colony became the second successful English colony in America. The first, Virginia's Jamestown, was mostly merchants and fortune-seekers. But the Pilgrims set out to build a new society guided by their religious principles. Thousands of other Puritans soon saw the opportunity to start a new life in America, where they could worship the way they wanted to.

The Massachusetts Bay Colony they formed was supposed to be "a city upon a hill," an example for the rest of the world.[2] They would eventually say the same thing about Massachusetts's capital city of Boston, and Boston native US president John F. Kennedy would later use the phrase to refer to the entire nation.

But Massachusetts wasn't the only English colony, and many of the other twelve colonies were also formed with a predominant religion. Some even had official state religions, the exact thing the First Amendment would be written to prevent!

The other New England colonies—Connecticut, Rhode Island, and New Hampshire—were also mainly Puritan. William Penn, the founder of the Pennsylvania Colony, was a devout Quaker and brought many Quakers with him. New York, New Jersey, and Delaware were melting pots of Presbyterians, Quakers, Catholics, Jews, and many others. Maryland was originally formed as a haven for Catholics, but the Church of England was

The Founders include all the signers of the original US Constitution, as well as influential Americans like Thomas Jefferson.

enshrined as state law there—as it was through several of the mid-Atlantic and southern colonies.[3]

The Original Constitution: Inclusion by Exclusion

At first, the Constitution mentioned religion only once. At the end of Article 6, it says that "no religious Test shall ever be required as a Qualification to any Office or public Trust under the United States."[4] That means no government job—from postal worker to president—can ever require the person doing it to practice any particular religion. But there's a big difference between making it illegal to force government workers into a particular religion and guaranteeing everyone freedom of religion.

That kind of difference—whether the government can only do what the Constitution allows or if it can do anything but what the Constitution forbids—is a big source of disagreement among scholars, judges, and

Banning Native and African religions

Freedom of religion hasn't always been guaranteed to all Americans, let alone everybody in America. A lot of the Constitution's original protections were just for white men.

Almost as soon as European colonists reached America they began expanding west, taking land from the Native Americans already living there. To keep natives from banding together and fighting to take their land back, the United States began outlawing their religions.[5] It wasn't until 1978 that Congress granted full First Amendment protection to Native American religious spaces, places, customs, and objects.[6]

Enslaved Africans—captured, transported and put to hard labor by force—didn't have any freedom. Africans taken from many different nations and tribes were widely forced to convert to their masters' religions. In many cases, they blended their ancestors' beliefs with Christian symbols and teachings.

lawyers today. It was just as big of an argument when the Founders wrote the Constitution in the first place.

Many of the thirteen colonies, when writing their own constitutions, settled questions about citizens' rights by including a list of protected freedoms right up front. But the Founders couldn't agree on whether to do the same thing in the national version. They argued about the idea at length during the Constitutional Convention—and even after the Constitution was adopted, many of the original Founders started the argument all over again as newly elected members of the first-ever Congress.[7]

James Madison wrote much of the original Constitution. He signed it thinking it was clear enough about people's rights and responsibilities that Congress didn't need to add a spelled-out list. But as a member of Congress, he came to think it would be better if the Constitution protected what he called "inalienable rights,"[8] personal freedoms no law or tax should be able to take away. Madison wrote out a series of seventeen amendments and introduced them to Congress to be debated and adopted.

The very first inalienable right in Madison's First Amendment? Freedom of religion.

Ten of Madison's seventeen amendments were ratified by the states, making what we now call the Bill of Rights the law of the land. But Madison was far from the only member of Congress who cared about making sure people wouldn't have to worry about the government outlawing their religion.

Thomas Jefferson's Virginian Vision

Before Thomas Jefferson wrote the Declaration of Independence, he drafted the constitution of his home colony, Virginia. Baptists and certain other Protestant groups there felt oppressed by the Anglican majority. Jefferson pushed the state government to protect religious minorities,

Thomas Jefferson's strong arguments for religious freedom informed the Bill of Rights' protections.

and in 1786 he wrote Virginia's Statute for Religious Freedom.[9] Before, during, and after the drafting of the US Constitution, Jefferson argued the national government should protect all citizens' religious rights the same way Virginia did:

> *No man shall be compelled to frequent or support any religious worship, place, or ministry whatsoever, nor shall be enforced, restrained, molested, or burthened in his body or goods, nor shall otherwise suffer on account of his religious opinions or belief; but that all men shall be free to profess, and by argument to maintain, their opinion in matters of religion, and that the same shall in no wise diminish, enlarge, or affect their civil capacities.*

After his religious freedom bill became law, Jefferson proudly wrote that his statute included "within the mantle of its protection, the Jew, the Gentile, the Christian and the Mahometan, the Hindoo and Infidel of every denomination."[10]

Madison wasn't as specifically inclusive when he wrote the First Amendment. He basically said the government can't make a law that either creates a religion or stops anyone from being religious:

> *Congress shall make no law respecting an establishment of religion, or prohibiting the free exercise thereof.*

This passage is often called the Establishment Clause. Figuring out exactly what Madison and the other framers meant by it is a challenge the Supreme Court still struggles with today.

It's a good thing Jefferson wrote a lot about how he (and his follow Founders) interpreted that clause! Jefferson wrote a letter to a group of

Baptists in Connecticut describing the Establishment Clause as "building a wall of separation between church and state."[11]

That phrase, "separation of church and state," is one people often cite when talking about religious freedom. In fact, the Supreme Court cited it while deciding an 1878 case, *Reynolds v. United States*.[12]

"It may be accepted almost as an authoritative declaration of the scope and effect of the [first] amendment," the majority opinion read. Other major cases would eventually be decided by reading the Establishment Clause that way. One of them, 1948's *McCollum v. Board of Education*, stopped public schools from teaching students how to practice religion.

Four years later, the court decided public school students could be released from school during school hours to study religion at a private school. In that decision, *Zorach v. Clauson*, the court held that "we are a religious people," and that our laws are written with the idea that a "Supreme Being" exists. [13]

So which is it? Is America a country founded by and for religious people? Or is it a place where everyone is free to worship—or not worship—however they want?

The answer is both.

2

Decisions, Decisions

Spend long enough thinking about guaranteed religious freedom and a thought might occur to you: What if someone started the First Church of Robbing Banks? Is a person's freedom to believe whatever they want more important than our regular criminal laws? The Establishment Clause doesn't say—and when the Constitution isn't clear or specific on something, it's up to the Supreme Court to decide how the words that define our country are really defined.

All Rise!

The Supreme Court justices do that by carefully deciding which cases are brought before them, then making decisions and writing out their opinions—including why and how they *disagree* with each other. Courts and government agencies then use those decisions and written opinions to enforce the law.

In 1878, a Utah colony man named George Reynolds married someone while he was still married to someone else. At the time, the Church of Jesus Christ of Latter-Day Saints instructed its male members to take multiple wives. But marrying more than one person at a time was against federal

The Supreme Court of the United States is the country's ultimate interpreter of laws and justice.

law. Reynolds argued before the court that the law was unconstitutional; following his god's word was more important than following mere rules.

But as the court noted in its decision, if anyone can believe whatever they want and beliefs are more important than law, that would "permit every citizen to become a law unto himself," and government would "exist only in name."[1]

Chief Justice Morrison Waite wrote the opinion for the court, which unanimously decided that individual beliefs didn't surpass federal law. In it, Waite cited part of a letter Jefferson wrote to the Danbury Baptist Association:

Believing with you that religion is a matter which lies solely between man and his God; that he owes account to none other for his faith or his worship; that the legislative powers of the government reach actions only, and not opinions,—I contemplate with sovereign reverence that act of the whole American people which declared that their legislature should "make no law respecting an establishment of religion or prohibiting the free exercise thereof," thus building a wall of separation between church and State.

Though the words "separation of church and state" don't appear anywhere in the Constitution, they set a standard that future courts would follow—and an easy way for citizens to understand what the Establishment Clause was supposed to establish.

Note that Jefferson wrote the government can legislate "actions only, and not opinions." Someone is free to believe whatever they want to believe—but if they want to live in American society, they still have to follow our laws.

So who wins when one person's freedom of religion conflicts with another's? What responsibility does the government have to step in?

Cantwell v. Connecticut

Another landmark case, *Cantwell v. Connecticut*, further defined these boundaries and in the process ensured state governments don't interfere with federally guaranteed rights.

In 1940, three Jehovah's Witnesses named Newton, Jesse, and Russell Cantwell went into a mainly Catholic neighborhood and began speaking to people about their faith—and against organized religions like Catholicism. They approached people on the street and played a recording of an anti-Catholic message over a speaker. Two angry people called the police, and the Jehovah's Witnesses were found guilty of disturbing

Jehovah's Witnesses can talk to people about their religious beliefs, even if their message isn't welcome.

the peace and soliciting without first getting permission from the local government.

"The [First] Amendment embraces two concepts," Justice Owen Roberts wrote in the unanimous decision in favor of the Cantwells: "freedom to believe and freedom to act."[2] Though a person's freedom to act on their beliefs is limited—again, there can't be a Church of Bank Robbing—Roberts and the rest of the court held that the government can't play any role in deciding religious truth.

In the case of the Cantwells, that meant local officials couldn't issue (or deny) permits to go around and talk to people based on the officials' ideals of appropriate religious beliefs. The reason? The Fourteenth Amendment, which ensures all Americans have equal protection under the law.

The First Amendment protects your freedom of religion just as much in Connecticut as it does everywhere else, and *Cantwell v. Connecticut* was the case that proved it.

The ruling also clarified that people have a right to peaceful expression of ideas, even when those ideas might offend other people around them.

Freedom of Religion, or Freedom from Religion?

People who want religion to play a bigger role in American life often say that "freedom of religion doesn't mean freedom from religion." That's true! Americans have the right to pray, wear religious symbols, and observe religious traditions basically wherever and whenever they want.

But that's equally true for all religions. Americans also have the right not to pray, not to wear religious symbols, and not to observe religious traditions. Our government can't interfere with anyone's beliefs, but it also can't encourage anyone to join any particular religion or even look like it's promoting one religion over others.

The Three-Pronged Lemon Test

The year 1971 brought us *Lemon v. Kurtzman*, the case that gave us the so-called Lemon Test. Rhode Island and Pennsylvania passed laws that gave extra money to private schoolteachers whose salaries didn't meet state averages.

Though teachers receiving the money weren't allowed to teach subjects or use textbooks that weren't okay for public schools, the court ruled that the states' laws were unconstitutional.

Over 95 percent of non-public-school kids went to religious schools, and nearly all of those were Roman Catholic. Even though no public money was supposed to fund religious classes or lessons, the law acted as direct support of the Catholic Church. Worse, the court said, the state would have to spend time and money tracking and policing the use of its money in these schools.

All of this added up to "excessive government entanglement,"[3] in the words of Chief Justice Warren E. Burger, which violates the third prong of his proposed three-pronged standard:[4]

Teachers are free to work at private religious schools, but the US government can't pay their wages.

1. The government's action must have a secular legislative purpose;
2. The government's action must not have the primary effect of either advancing or inhibiting religion; and
3. The government's action must not result in an "excessive government entanglement" with religion.

"Secular" means not having to do with religion—and in this case, the two states' laws passed the test: making sure all teachers are paid fairly has nothing to do religion. The court didn't specifically pass or fail the laws on the second proposed prong, but it flunked the laws hard on the third one.

The US government isn't in the business of funding, promoting, or regulating religion—and it's almost impossible for public funds to go to private schools without doing at least one of the above.

Passing the Lemon Test

Everyone in America is always allowed to pray. The Supreme Court has repeatedly said that no law can force anyone to worship, or stop anyone from worshipping, in their hearts. No matter where or when you are in this country, it's always okay to have faith.

As decided in *Cantwell v. Connecticut*, it's also always okay to talk about your beliefs, as long as you're being peaceful and not disruptive. But there are limits on how we act on our beliefs—and there are definitely rules about how religion is expressed in public and private settings.

Religion in School

The phrase "school prayer" is often used, misleadingly, as a controversial discussion topic: "Should prayer be allowed in schools?" But there's no real controversy here: individual students are always allowed to pray in schools.

The Good News Club

In 2001's *Good News Club v. Milford Central School District*, the court said that straight-up religious groups are allowed to meet on school grounds, as long as it's outside of school hours. When the Milford, NY, school district

Students are always allowed to pray in school, but how does that impact wider activities on school grounds?

If a public school's facilities are available for public use, they have to be available for everyone to use.

denied the Christian education group Good News Club permission to use its otherwise open-to-the-public facilities, Justice Clarence Thomas wrote "Milford's restriction violates the Club's free speech rights and that no Establishment Clause concern justifies that violation."[1]

Because Milford had been allowing all kinds of groups to use its buildings and spaces when school was out, denying the Good News Club the opportunity to do the same wasn't just a too-strict application of the Lemon Test. The court held that the school district actually violated the club's First Amendment rights!

This idea, that a public place has to let all groups have equal access, is important. If the government can stop a group from using a public facility because of its religious beliefs, that could be a step down the road toward banning that religion altogether.

But the government can't promote one religion over another or even appear like it's doing so. That's why *group* prayer in public schools is almost always unconstitutional.

Graduating Prayers

In *Lee v. Weisman*, a Providence, RI, middle-school principal invited a rabbi to speak at his school's graduation ceremony. Daniel Weisman's daughter was among the graduates, and he objected to prayers being included in a

A graduation can be thought of as a sacred event, but including a prayer means excluding some students.

public school function.[2] He filed for a temporary restraining order preventing the prayer, and his application was denied. After the ceremony, where the rabbi did speak, Weisman sought a permanent restraining order banning all Providence schools from inviting clergy to lead prayers or speak benedictions at school events.

In a close (5-4) decision, the court ruled that a religious official leading assembled students in prayer created "a state-sponsored and state-directed religious exercise in a public school."[3] Even though the student wouldn't have had to say the prayer—and nobody can really make anyone pray—all of a student's classmates rising and speaking along with a clergy-led prayer would make any student feel like they were supposed to be praying, too.

"It is a cornerstone principle of our Establishment Clause jurisprudence that it is no part of the business of government to compose official prayers for any group of the American people to recite as a part of a religious program carried on by government," wrote Justice Anthony Kennedy, "and that is what the school officials attempted to do."[4]

Even though school officials directed the rabbi to make the prayer as non-prayer-like as possible, that made it worse: The school "directed and controlled" the content of the prayer, increasing the government's entanglement with the religious event.

If the problem is school officials controlling the prayer, and students are allowed to pray, can students lead other students in prayer?

Game Day Prayers

In 1995, the court heard *Santa Fe Independent School District v. Doe*, a case where the student council chaplain had recited a Christian prayer before each home football game. A Mormon family and a Catholic family sued the school district, which quickly changed the policy so that any student

"Under God"

The first version of the Pledge of Allegiance was written after the Civil War, by Union army captain George T. Balch. It was revised in 1892 by a socialist minister named Francis Bellamy. The pledge wasn't recognized by Congress until 1942, and the words "under God" weren't added until 1954.[5]

In 1943, the Supreme Court ruled that students couldn't be forced to salute the flag.[6] In 2002, the Ninth Circuit Court of Appeals held that the phrase "under God" made leading the pledge in public schools unconstitutional—but in 2004 the Supreme Court overturned this, since the parent who brought the complaint didn't live with his child. Since then, multiple challenges have maintained that "under God" is fine to be included in the pledge but that students can't be forced to speak it or stand for it.

could lead any prayer, as long as it wasn't trying to convert other students to their religion.

The school district then put it up to the students to vote whether A) there would be a prayer, and B) which students would say it. That meant the majority would rule, and students with minority viewpoints wouldn't be represented. Even with private students leading the prayers instead of public officials, the government can't support or promote one religion over another.

As Justice John Paul Stevens wrote for the 6–3 majority, "The delivery of a message such as the invocation here—on school property, at school-sponsored events, over the school's public address system, by a speaker representing the student body, under the supervision of school faculty, and pursuant to a school policy that explicitly and implicitly encourages public prayer—is not properly characterized as 'private' speech."

But what happens when religious expression is done on private property—and it impacts somcone else?

"Under God" wasn't added to the Pledge of Allegiance until 1954.
Students cannot be forced to stand for the pledge.

Religion at Work

Remember how the Supreme Court ruled that the Good News Club's freedom of religion couldn't be denied? And that churches and other religious organizations are exempt from many rules that bind public bodies like schools? In *Burwell v. Hobby Lobby*, federal courts recognized the right of family-owned for-profit companies to act in accordance with that family's belief.

As part of the Affordable Care Act, companies were required to provide health insurance plans that (among many other things) covered expenses for birth control. The family that owns Hobby Lobby, a national retail chain with over eight hundred stores,[7] decided some of those medicines were against their religious beliefs and refused to contribute to covering their cost.

In a controversial 5–4 decision, the Supreme Court ruled that Congress's 1993 Religious Freedom Restoration Act was intended to apply to corporations, as well as people—and federal laws shouldn't force family-owned for-profit companies to violate that family's religious beliefs, just as they shouldn't do so for religious nonprofits.[8]

In the years that followed, legal battles surrounding the Affordable Care Act's contraceptive mandate continued. In 2017, a federal injunction blocked a Trump administration order that would make it much easier to opt out of providing birth-control coverage.[9]

Though this case might have opened up a flood of cases where businesses deprived employees of benefits based on purported religious freedom, the University of Utah found no significant change in the frequency of religious-liberty cases brought before US courts since *Burwell v. Hobby Lobby*.[10]

What stops a company from deciding that providing any kind of insurance at all is against its religious beliefs? Or paying workers money? The same thing that stops people from founding the First Church of Bank Robbing: The law of the land can't guarantee people the right to break the law.

But what if the religious liberty case *involves* a court—and a judge who thinks God gave him the right to break the law?

Religion in Government

In 2001, Roy Moore, then the chief justice of the Alabama Supreme Court, had a 2.5-ton granite monument of the Ten Commandments put in the main room of Alabama's judicial building. Moore publicly said the monument was meant to show off his belief that God's law was the "moral foundation" of US law—and then he refused to obey a court order to remove it.[11]

Moore not only insisted his religious beliefs were more important than the Constitution, he also insisted that being the chief justice of Alabama's Supreme Court meant he could decide whether or not he needed to obey federal court orders.

The Eleventh Circuit Court of Appeals decided that not only did Moore's monument fail two of the three prongs of the Lemon Test, Moore could not rule himself above the law.

"In the final analysis, the concept of law and order, the very essence of a republican form of government, embraces the notion that when the judicial process of a state or federal court, acting within the sphere of its competence, has been exhausted and has resulted in a final judgment, all persons affected thereby are obliged to obey it," the decision read. "If necessary, the court order will be enforced. The rule of law will prevail."

Not only was the monument removed from the courthouse, Moore was removed from his position on Alabama's Supreme Court.[12]

Your Arm vs. My Nose

From Thomas Jefferson's vision to the Lemon Test, our Constitution's words—and the way the Supreme Court interprets them—forbid the government from even making it seem like it prefers one faith over another. The idea that our government could ban a whole religion sounds ridiculous.

So how did President Trump enact a "Muslim ban"?

The Travel Ban

During his campaign, President Donald Trump repeatedly spoke about the threat he thought America faced from "radical Islamic terrorism."[1] In 2015, he called for a "total and complete shutdown of Muslims entering the United States."[2]

Such a shutdown would be unconstitutional. Remember, even before the Bill of Rights was adopted, the Constitution said "no religious test" could be a requirement for holding a public job in America—and Trump wanted to require a religious test to even *enter* America.

Exactly one week after his January 20, 2017, inauguration, Trump signed Executive Order 13769, which, among other restrictions, blocked

The so-called Muslim ban, and the Supreme Court decision upholding parts of it, remain controversial.

the entry of travelers from Iran, Iraq, Libya, Somalia, Sudan, Syria, and Yemen. People were detained at the airport, families were stranded apart, thousands of valid visas were revoked, and enforcement seemed to vary wildly across different US ports of entry.

Less than a week later, a nationwide restraining order was granted in the case of *Washington v. Trump*, stopping its enforcement. This restraining order was then upheld by the Court of Appeals for the Ninth Circuit. On March 6, 2017, Trump's administration tried again; he signed Executive Order 13780, which had a more limited scope and fewer restrictions on refugees.

Again, the order was challenged—and at first, the courts struck it down. Judge Derek Watson of Hawaii ruled that Trump's public statements and social media posts showed that he intended to ban people with Muslim beliefs from entering the country and that these executive orders were that ban.

"A reasonable, objective observer," he wrote, "would conclude that the Executive Order was issued with a purpose to disfavor a particular religion."[3] The Court of Appeals for both the Fourth Circuit and Ninth Circuit agreed. During this time, Trump also signed two presidential proclamations[4] changing who was affected by the travel ban—softening some restrictions, but broadening others.

But when the case, *Hawaii v. Trump*, reached the Supreme Court, Chief Justice John Roberts wrote for a 5-4 majority in Trump's favor. Roberts's opinion said Trump's campaign statements didn't change the fact that the president has the authority to change immigration standards and guidelines.

"Plaintiffs argue that this President's words strike at fundamental standards of respect and tolerance, in violation of our constitutional tradition," Roberts wrote. "But the issue before us is not whether to denounce the statements. It is instead the significance of those statements in reviewing

Opponents of the travel ban wait outside the Supreme Court building for the decision on *Hawaii v. Trump*.

Pastafarians

Have you heard of the Flying Spaghetti Monster? Pastafarians would like you to think they believe it created the universe.

A Kansas parent named Bobby Henderson got upset about the state's public schools teaching "intelligent design" and demanded schools also teach that the world might have been made by a flying spaghetti monster.

Nonreligious people everywhere now use the Flying Spaghetti Monster to point out the privileges society provides to people of faith.

Stephen Cavanaugh sued to get accommodations for his "FSMism" while in prison, forcing a federal judge to rule that "it is not a 'religion' within the meaning of the relevant federal statutes." However, multiple Pastafarians have convinced state governments to allow them to wear pasta strainers on their heads in their driver's license photos, thanks to rules allowing religious headgear.

a Presidential directive, neutral on its face, addressing a matter within the core of executive responsibility. In doing so, we must consider not only the statements of a particular President, but also the authority of the Presidency itself."[5]

Roberts, though, pointed out this authority does have limits. He condemned the court's World War II–era ruling on *Korematsu v. United States*, the Supreme Court decision that let the government round up people of Japanese descent and put them in internment camps. Because no administration has tried anything like that again, the court has never had a chance to overturn its previous ruling.

"The forcible relocation of U.S. citizens to concentration camps, solely and explicitly on the basis of race, is objectively unlawful and outside the scope of presidential authority," Roberts wrote. "*Korematsu* was gravely wrong the day it was decided, has been overruled in the court of history, and—to be clear—'has no place in law under the Constitution.'"

If rounding up people from a certain culture and putting them in detention camps is obviously wrong and unlawful, but it's okay to keep out people from countries where a certain culture is dominant, it's no wonder many people are scared about how much further the government can go before it crosses the line.

Even as President Trump continues to crack down on immigration and refugees, many white, Christian Americans feel like they're the ones being threatened.

Masterpiece Cakeshop

Some Christians consider same-sex relationships and marriage to be against their religious beliefs. As American laws and courts increasingly decide that jobs, housing, marriage, and other civil rights can't be denied to someone based on their sexual orientation or identity, the Supreme Court will have to decide which is more important: LGBTQ Americans' right to equal protection under the law or other Americans' right to believe religious teachings that being LGBTQ is wrong?

In *Masterpiece Cakeshop v. Colorado Civil Rights Commission*, the court had an opportunity to decide—and didn't.

In 2012, Charlie Craig and David Mullins went to Masterpiece Cakeshop in Lakewood, CO, to commission a wedding cake from owner Jack Phillips. Phillips declined, saying same-sex marriage is against his religious beliefs.

This case raises many tricky issues. Many see cake decorating as an art; can a court legally force an artist to make something that goes against their beliefs? But if Phillips can deny service to gay people, wouldn't that mean any store could deny service to gay people? What if Phillips thought God did not want him to make cakes for people who weren't the same religion as him; would discriminating against people based on religion be okay?

Masterpiece Cakeshop owner Jack Phillips, who refused to make a same-sex wedding cake, at work

The court didn't answer any of these questions. In a 7–2 ruling, the court decided that the Colorado Civil Rights Commission, who handled the discrimination complaint, didn't give Phillips's beliefs full and fair consideration.

"The outcome of cases like this in other circumstances must await further elaboration in the courts," Chief Justice Roberts wrote for the majority, "all in the context of recognizing that these disputes must be resolved with tolerance, without undue disrespect to sincere religious beliefs, and without subjecting gay persons to indignities when they seek goods and services in an open market."[6]

For many people worried about the future of religious freedom in the United States, that "further elaboration" can't come soon enough.

The Religious Liberty Task Force

In June 2018, the then attorney general Jeff Sessions announced he was forming a "Religious Liberty Task Force" while speaking at a religious liberty summit held by the federal Department of Justice. Sessions warned that American culture had become "less hospitable to people of faith" and his new task force would ensure federal prosecutors were following his guidelines when deciding which cases to bring to court.[7]

At the lowest level, that results in cases like churches being allowed to support political candidates (even though the law says they can't do that and remain a tax-exempt nonprofit). At the highest level, it will mean more opportunities for the Supreme Court to make landmark decisions like *Cantwell v. Connecticut* and *Good News Club v. Milford Central School District.*

Debate will continue about the role religion plays in our private and public lives. The Constitution guarantees our right to believe (or not) however we want and express those beliefs—even if others find them offensive, as in *Cantwell*. Technology and social media have made this more true than ever before, as we're free to express ourselves to the entire world.

There's an old saying: "Your right to swing your arm stops when it hits my nose." Over the centuries our still-young nation has existed, this much has been clear: the United States government cannot tell you what to believe or not to believe. That also means it can't promote any particular religion, nor outlaw any particular religion.

As Jefferson wrote: no one shall "suffer on account of his religious opinions or belief; but that all men shall be free to profess, and by argument to maintain, their opinion in matters of religion."

Chapter Notes

Introduction

1. "US Constitution: The First Amendment," Legal Information Institute, https://www.law.cornell.edu/constitution/first_amendment.
2. "Masterpiece Cakeshop, Ltd., Et Al., v. Colorado Civil Rights Commission, Et Al.," Supreme Court of the United States, https://www.supremecourt.gov/opinions/17pdf/16-111_j4el.pdf.
3. "Timeline of the Muslim Ban," ACLU-wa.org, https://www.aclu-wa.org/pages/timeline-muslim-ban.
4. Tara Isabella Burton, "Jeff Sessions Announces a Religious Liberty Task Force to Combat 'Dangerous' Secularism," Vox.com, July 31, 2018, https://www.vox.com/identities/2018/7/31/17631110/jeff-sessions-religious-liberty-task-force-memo-christian-nationalism.

Chapter One: The First Amendment

1. "Why the Pilgrim Fathers Left England," BBC, January 18, 1998, http://news.bbc.co.uk/2/hi/uk_news/47688.stm.
2. John Winthrop, "A Modell of Christian Charity," 1630, Hanover College, https://history.hanover.edu/texts/winthmod.html.
3. "13 Colonies Chart," FacingHistory.org, https://www.facinghistory.org/nobigotry/religion-colonial-america-trends-regulations-and-beliefs.
4. US Constitution," Cornell University, https://www.law.cornell.edu/constitution.
5. Michael P. Guéno, "Native Americans, Law, and Religion in America," Oxford Research Encyclopedias, November 2017, http://religion.oxfordre.com/view/10.1093/acrefore/9780199340378.001.0001/acrefore-9780199340378-e-140.
6. American Indian Religious Freedom Act," Office for Coastal Management, NOAA, https://coast.noaa.gov/data/Documents/OceanLawSearch/

Summary%20of%20Law%20-%20American%20Indian%20Religious%20Freedom%20Act.pdf.

7. Gordon Lloyd, "The Constitutional Framers and the Bill of Rights," TeachingAmericanHistory.org, http://teachingamericanhistory.org/bor/themes/framers.

8. "Jump Back in Time," Library of Congress, http://www.americaslibrary.gov/jb/nation/jb_nation_bofright_2.html.

9. "Thomas Jefferson and the Virginia Statute for Religious Freedom," Virginia Museum of History and Culture, https://www.virginia-history.org/collections-and-resources/virginia-history-explorer/thomas-jefferson.

10. Kenneth C. Davis, "America's True History of Religious Tolerance," *Smithsonian*, October 2010, https://www.smithsonianmag.com/history/americas-true-history-of-religious-tolerance-61312684/?=&no-ist=&page=1.

11. "Jefferson's Letter to the Danbury Baptists," Library of Congress, https://www.loc.gov/loc/lcib/9806/danpre.html.

12. "Reynolds v. United States," Oyez, https://www.oyez.org/cases/1850-1900/98us145.

13. "Zorach v. Clauson," Oyez, https://www.oyez.org/cases/1940-1955/343us306.

Chapter Two: Decisions, Decisions

1. "Reynolds v. United States (1879)," Bill of Rights Institute, https://billofrightsinstitute.org/educate/educator-resources/lessons-plans/landmark-supreme-court-cases-elessons/reynolds-v-united-states-1878.

2. Brian P. Smentkowski, "Owen Josephus Roberts, United States Jurist," *Encyclopedia Britannica*, https://www.britannica.com/biography/Owen-Josephus-Roberts.

3. "Lemon v. Kurtzmann," Cornell Law School, https://www.law.cornell.edu/supremecourt/text/403/602.

4. "Lemon Test Law and Legal Definition," USLegal.com, https://definitions.uslegal.com/l/lemon-test.

Chapter Three: Passing the Lemon Test

1. "Good News Club v. Milford Central School," Oyez, https://www.oyez.org/cases/2000/99-2036.

2. Ralph D. Mawdsley, "Lee v. Weisman," *Encyclopedia Britannica*, https://www.britannica.com/topic/Lee-v-Weisman.

3. "Lee v. Weisman," Oyez, https://www.oyez.org/cases/1991/90-1014.

4. "Lee v. Weisman," Cornell Law School, https://www.law.cornell.edu/supremecourt/text/505/577.

5. Sandy Hingston, "11 Things You Might Not Know About the Pledge of Allegiance," *Philly* Magazine, September 8, 2016, https://www.phillymag.com/news/2016/09/08/11-things-pledge-of-allegiance.

6. "West Virginia State Board of Education v. Barnette," Oyez, https://www.oyez.org/cases/1940-1955/319us624.

7. "Our Story," Hobby Lobby, https://www.hobbylobby.com/about-us/our-story.

8. "Burwell v. Hobby Lobby," Oyez, https://www.oyez.org/cases/2013/13-354.

9. Robert Pear, "Court Temporarily Blocks Trump Order Against Contraceptive Coverage," *New York Times*, December 15, 2017, https://www.nytimes.com/2017/12/15/us/politics/obamacare-birth-control-trump.html.

10. Luke W. Goodrich and Rachel N. Busick, "Sex, Drugs, and Eagle Feathers: An Empirical Study of Federal Religious Freedom Cases," *Seton Hall Law Review*, February 18, 2018, https://papers.ssrn.com/sol3/papers.cfm?abstract_id=3067053##.

11. Jonathon H. Adler, "Kim Davis and the Case of Justice Moore," *Washington Post*, September 4, 2015, https://www.washingtonpost.

com/news/volokh-conspiracy/wp/2015/09/04/kim-davis-and-the-case-of-justice-moore/?utm_term=.e9bde1fa6c13

12. "Ten Commandments Judge Removed from Office," CNN, November 14, 2003, http://www.cnn.com/2003/LAW/11/13/moore.tencommandments.

Chapter Four: Your Arm vs. My Nose

1. Zack Beauchamp, "Trump Loves Saying 'Radical Islamic Terrorism.' He Has a Tough Time with 'White Supremacy,'" Vox, August 14, 2017, https://www.vox.com/world/2017/8/14/16143634/trump-charlottesville-white-supremacy-terrorism-islamism.

2. Jenna Johnson, "Trump Calls for 'Total and Complete Shutdown of Muslims Entering the United States,'" *Washington Post*, December 7, 2015, https://www.washingtonpost.com/news/post-politics/wp/2015/12/07/donald-trump-calls-for-total-and-complete-shutdown-of-muslims-entering-the-united-states/?utm_term=.4d094dabcdef.

3. Dan Levine and Mica Rosenberg, "Hawaii Judge Halts Trump's New Travel Ban Before It Can Go into Effect," Reuters, March 15, 2017, https://www.reuters.com/article/us-usa-immigration-court-idUSKBN16M17N.

4. "Timeline of the Muslim Ban," ACLU Washington, https://www.aclu-wa.org/pages/timeline-muslim-ban.

5. "Hawaii v. Trump," Oyez, https://www.oyez.org/cases/2017/17-965.

6. "Masterpiece Cakeshop, Ltd. v. Colorado Civil Rights Commission," Oyez, https://www.oyez.org/cases/2017/16-111.

7. Tara Isabella Burton, "Jeff Sessions Announces a Religious Liberty Task Force to Combat 'Dangerous' Secularism," Vox, July 31, 2018, https://www.vox.com/identities/2018/7/31/17631110/jeff-sessions-religious-liberty-task-force-memo-christian-nationalism.

Glossary

article A paragraph or section of any writing, for example, referencing the sections of the Constitution of the United States.

cite To make reference to a decision in another case to make a legal point in argument.

Constitutional Convention A 1787 convention of politicians that drew up the Constitution of the United States.

court A group of judges that administer justice.

dissent An explicit disagreement by one or more judges with the decision of the majority on a case. Important Supreme Court decisions often have strong dissenting opinions written by the judges in the minority.

Founders A general name for male American patriots during the Revolutionary War, especially the signers of the Declaration of Independence and those who drafted the Constitution.

invocation The act of invoking or calling upon a deity, spirit, etc., for aid, protection, inspiration, or the like.

jurisprudence A body or a system of laws.

majority opinion The decision on a court case with which most deciding judges agree. Supreme Court majority opinions help set important guidelines for all other US courts to follow.

mandate A command or an authorization to act. In this book, it refers to a law that forces insurance providers to pay for certain medicine.

nonprofit A group that does not have to pay taxes because it is a "public charity" formed to provide "public benefit."

GLOSSARY

organized religion A belief system that has large numbers of followers and a set of rules that must be followed.

secular Something related to the physical world; not overtly or specifically religious.

statute A law enacted by the legislative branch of a government.

unanimous Having the agreement and consent of all; being of one mind; for example a Supreme Court decision that all the justices agree on.

Further Reading

Books

Barcella, Laura. *Know Your Rights!: A Modern Kid's Guide to the American Constitution.* New York, NY: Sterling Children's Books, 2018.

Demuth, Patricia Brennan. *What Is the Constitution?* New York, NY: Penguin Workshop, 2018

Levinson, Cynthia. *Fault Lines in the Constitution: The Framers, Their Fights, and the Flaws that Affect Us Today.* Atlanta, GA: Peachtree Publishers, 2017.

Websites

Ducksters US Government for Kids

www.ducksters.com/history/us_government/first_amendment.php

This site is devoted to history, science, geography, and more.

USConstitution.Net

www.usconstitution.net/constkids4.html

The fourth- to seventh-grade section of this site is dedicated to understanding the US Constitution.

Index